10/98

24.98

10/98

24.98

GREAT BUILDINGS

THE COLOSSEUM

Peter Chrisp

RSVP
RAINTREE
STECK·VAUGHN
PUBLISHERS
The Steck-Vaughn Company

Austin, Texas

GREAT BUILDINGS

THE COLOSSEUM

THE EMPIRE STATE BUILDING

THE GREAT PYRAMID

THE HOUSES OF PARLIAMENT

THE PARTHENON

THE TAJ MAHAL

Published by Raintree Steck-Vaughn Publishers,
an imprint of Steck-Vaughn Company

Library of Congress Cataloging-in-Publication Data
Chrisp, Peter.
The Colosseum / Peter Chrisp.
    p.   cm.—(Great buildings)
    Includes bibliographical references and index.
    Summary: Discusses the history, construction, and the many uses of the Colosseum in Rome.
    ISBN 0-8172-4916-8
    1. Rome, Ancient—Juvenile literature.
    [1. Rome, Ancient. 2. Architecture.]
    I. Title. II. Series.

Printed in Italy. Bound in the United States.
1 2 3 4 5 6 7 8 9 0 01 00 99 98 97

Illustrations: Francis Phillipps and Clive Spong
Map: Peter Bull

CONTENTS

▲ A Roman vase is decorated with an image of a gladiator contest. The gladiator on the right has lost the fight and is raising his finger to beg for mercy.

IN THE ARENA

Two men faced each other under the blazing sun. They were in the arena, the sand-covered fighting area, of a huge open-air building called an amphitheater. As the two circled each other, the shouts of 50,000 spectators echoed around the walls.

The hoplomachus carried a shield and sword and was protected by a helmet and armor. The retiarius, or net-man, had only a leather guard on his left arm; his weapons were a trident and a net. The hoplomachus was better protected, but his armor slowed him down. The retiarius was easier to wound, but he was fast on his feet.

Suddenly, the retiarius threw his net. The hoplomachus jumped aside, but lost his balance. The retiarius closed in quickly, jabbing at his enemy. The hoplomachus's weapons dropped onto the sand. He held a finger up in the air, asking for mercy. Some of the crowd shouted to finish off the loser. Others stuck their thumbs in the air, yelling, "Spare him! He fought bravely!" The final decision belonged to the Roman emperor, sitting in the front row. The fighters looked up at him, waiting to see what he would decide.

CHAPTER ONE

ROME AND THE ROMAN EMPIRE

▼ In the second century A.D., the Roman Empire was at its height. It included all the lands around the Mediterranean Sea. Between 50 and 90 million people —about one fifth of the world's population at the time—lived under Roman rule.

The gladiators' contest took place 2,000 years ago in the city of Rome. The Romans were rulers of a vast empire, which was made up of many countries. They had built up their empire because of their skill in battle. Once the soldiers had conquered a new land, the Roman government officials and tax collectors would arrive, together with builders, traders, and craftspeople. Everything that the Romans did was well organized, from fighting wars to ruling over the conquered peoples.

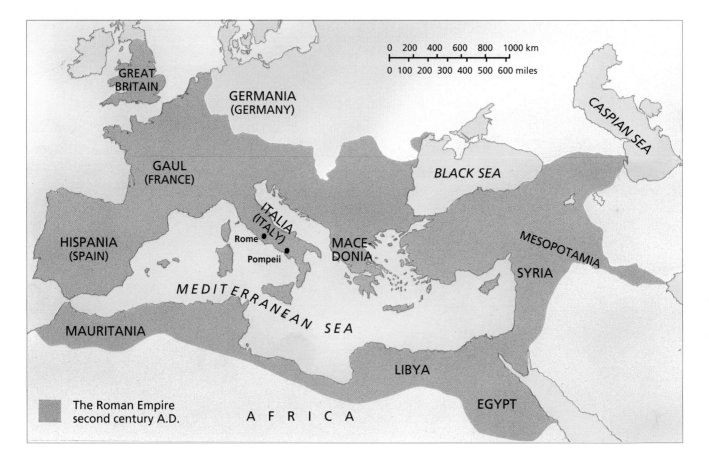

GREAT BRITAIN

GERMANIA (GERMANY)

CASPIAN SEA

0 200 400 600 800 1000 km
0 100 200 300 400 500 600 miles

GAUL (FRANCE)

BLACK SEA

ITALIA (ITALY)

Rome

Pompeii

MACE-DONIA

MESOPOTAMIA

HISPANIA (SPAIN)

SYRIA

MEDITERRANEAN SEA

MAURITANIA

LIBYA

EGYPT

The Roman Empire second century A.D.

AFRICA

▼ Slaves were treated as property, like horses or cattle. They could be bought and sold or killed if their owners wished. However, this slave carrying a tray of food was included in a floor mosaic, which even shows his name.

Throughout the empire, people came to share the Roman way of life. In places as far apart as Great Britain in the northwest and Egypt in the southeast, people dressed in similar clothes and worshiped the same Roman gods. They did their shopping with Roman coins and ate their meals from Roman pottery. People spoke one of two languages: In the western countries it was Latin, and in the east it was Greek.

Within the empire, there were different groups of people with different rights. At the top were the Roman citizens. In the first century A.D., there were about six million of them. Far more people made up the second class of noncitizens. At the bottom were the slaves, people with no rights at all.

▶ The Romans were wonderful builders. Wherever they went, they built towns linked by long, straight roads. The Via Colosseo in Rome is still used by visitors to the Colosseum.

Rome, the capital of the empire, was an enormous place. In the first century A.D., more than a million people lived there. There were fashionable areas, where the rich lived in great mansions. There were also slums, where the poor people lived, crowded into tall blocks of cheaply built apartments.

The center of the city was filled with grand public buildings. There were temples to the various gods, such as Vesta and Jupiter, who were believed to protect the city and the empire. There were also enormous bath-houses, where people went to relax in the afternoons.

▼ This 19th century drawing shows the center of Rome as it was in A.D. 270. The Colosseum (1) is in the center of the background, with the Forum (2) to its left. You can see the huge Stadium of Domitian (3), which was used for chariot races, and the Circus Maximus (4), which could hold 250,000 people.

The biggest buildings of all were those used for public entertainment. The huge amphitheater, the Colosseum, in the center of the city, was the tallest building in Rome. The Romans were proud of their city. It was described by one writer, Seneca, as "the greatest and loveliest city in the world."

▼ The Forum was at the center of daily life for Romans. It was a meeting place and a market and included temples and government buildings. You can see the Colosseum behind the ruins of the Forum.

▼ Chariot races, held in huge stadia called circuses, were tremendously popular with the Romans. Here a four-horse chariot is approaching the three columns of the turning post. Just going around the post on horseback is the Jubilator, whose job it was to encourage the contestants.

The people of Rome were provided with a continuous round of entertainment such as chariot races, plays, and musical performances. Between one hundred and two hundred days of the year were public holidays, when the emperor put on free shows for the people.

The holidays were mainly religious festivals in honor of particular gods. There were also special shows to mark important events, such as a victory in war. The processions that formed part of these celebrations were great entertainments in themselves, with soldiers, musicians, and slaves carrying religious statues, followed by animals to be sacrificed to the gods.

Almost every large Roman town had an amphitheater, a place to see gladiators fighting. Fights between gladiators had started with the custom of killing prisoners of war or slaves at the funerals of rich Romans. This was a sacrifice to the spirit of the dead man. Later, slaves were forced to fight each other to the death at funerals. People enjoyed watching the fights, and they eventually turned into a form of entertainment.

▲ Some Roman amphitheaters, such as this one at Arles in France, are still used. If you look closely, you can see that the audience is watching a bullfight.

Roman citizens expected their emperor and nobles to provide them with these free amusements. The emperor was also expected to provide free food, particularly wheat, which was distributed every month. The shows and the food were needed to keep the thousands of poorer citizens happy and out of trouble. If an emperor failed to come up with either, there would be riots.

"The Roman people is held together by two things above all others—its food supplies and its shows."

Fronto, a Roman writer

► The dishes prepared for a Roman banquet to celebrate a religious festival or an important event. The mosaic shows a gazelle in the center, surrounded by vegetables, fruit, and fowl.

CHAPTER TWO

THE PLAN FOR THE COLOSSEUM

In A.D. 64, a terrible fire ripped its way through the heart of Rome. It burned for nine days before it was finally put out. When the Emperor Nero began to rebuild the city, he saved a huge area in the center for a new palace. In the entrance of the Golden House, as Nero called his palace, there was a colossus, or gigantic statue, of the emperor himself. It was 120 ft. (37 m) high and made of shining bronze. Outside, Nero had a private park with a lake.

A bust of Nero, who was the Roman emperor from A.D. 54 to A.D. 68, succeeding his stepfather Claudius when he was only 17 years old. He went on to become one of the most cruel emperors, killing mercilessly and ruling with tyranny. Nero plundered the Roman Empire to pay for his extravagances and was widely disliked.

The Golden House was hated by the people of Rome. At night, they wrote rude comments about their emperor and his palace on the walls of the city: "The palace is spreading and swallowing Rome!" Nero was already unpopular with many Romans. He was known to have murdered his mother, his wife, and his stepbrother. Now, when people saw how well he had done out of the fire, many wondered whether he had started the blaze himself.

Nero had barely moved into his new home when he learned of widespread uprisings against his rule. The generals commanding Rome's greatest armies refused to obey Nero's orders, saying that they would make better emperors themselves. Abandoned by everyone, Nero killed himself.

▲ Inside the Golden House, the rooms were richly decorated. The dining rooms had ceilings of carved ivory with sliding panels to allow flowers or perfume to be showered down on the guests. This is one of the few surviving rooms, where the decorations are still faintly visible.

A.D. 69—the year of many emperors
Nero's death was followed by 18 months of war as rival generals fought each other for power. One after another, three men became emperor in Rome, only to be overthrown and die in their turn. Their portraits are stamped on these Roman coins: Galba (left), Otho (middle), and Vitellius (right). Whenever possible, Roman emperors used coins to celebrate their own heroism and importance.

By the end of A.D. 69, there was a new emperor, an old general called Vespasian. In the previous 18 months, four Roman emperors had died. Vespasian did not want to to be the fifth dead emperor. For his own safety, he needed to be popular with the people of Rome.

Vespasian decided to pull down most of Nero's hated Golden House and to open the grounds as a public garden. On the site he also planned to build something for the people. A huge amphitheater for public shows would let everybody know that he was not going to be a selfish ruler like Nero. An amphitheater, a place for the people, made a wonderful contrast with Nero's private pleasure palace.

▶ The Emperor Vespasian, who ruled the Roman Empire from A.D. 69 until his death in A.D. 79, the year before the Colosseum was opened. Two of his sons became emperor after him: Titus (A.D. 79-81) and then Domitian (A.D. 81-96).

Vespasian died before the building was completed. It was opened in A.D. 80 by his son, the Emperor Titus. The Romans called their new amphitheater the Flavian Amphitheater, after the family name of Vespasian and Titus. The later name Colosseum comes from the colossus, the gigantic statue of Nero that stood next to it. It was such an impressive statue that it had not been destroyed by Vespasian, just renamed as a statue of the sun-god.

"Here, where the hated halls of a cruel king lately glistened, and one single house began to take over the whole city... Here, where Nero had his fish ponds, the vast body of the magnificent amphitheater now rises... Rome has been given back to herself."

Martial, a Roman poet

▲ A relief from the Arch of Titus in Rome shows the Emperor Titus in a procession after the Romans destroyed Jerusalem. Spoils from the temple of Jerusalem are carried in triumph.

CHAPTER THREE

BUILDING THE COLOSSEUM

Although amphitheaters had been built before, no one had ever built one as big as the Colosseum. The Emperor Vespasian wanted a building that could hold 50,000 spectators. The first step was to have a plan drawn up by an architect.

▼ The plan of the Colosseum (below) shows the overall shape as if you were looking down on it. The plan also shows entrances, columns, and tiers. The cross-section (right) shows a slice of the building as if seen from the side.

How would the architect make something big enough to hold all the people? It would have to be tall rather than wide, so that everyone would be close enough to see the gladiators. The problem with a tall building is that the weight of all the seating pushes outward. So the outer walls had to be strong to keep the building from collapsing.

Another problem was one of crowd control. How do you get 50,000 excited people safely into and out of an amphitheater? The answer was to have 76 different entrances, each with its own stairway to a seating area.

A Roman architect had to have many different skills. As well as designing the building, he was in charge of construction. He was like a general in charge of an army. There were hundreds of workers and materials to organize and supply. Each of the materials used—brick, concrete, limestone, marble, wood, and iron—was the specialty of a particular group of skilled craftsmen. There were also hundreds of unskilled workers, mostly slaves, to carry loads.

▲ This photograph taken from an airplane clearly shows the oval shape of the Colosseum. You can imagine how it would feel to be sitting high up in the amphitheater, looking down on the contest below.

Guilds

The craftsmen who built the Colosseum would have been members of a guild, which is a group of people all practicing the same craft. Stonecutters, bronzeworkers, brickmakers and bricklayers, concrete makers, and carpenters all would have worked on the Colosseum. They all would have had their own guild. This stone carving shows a smith beating metal on his anvil.

17

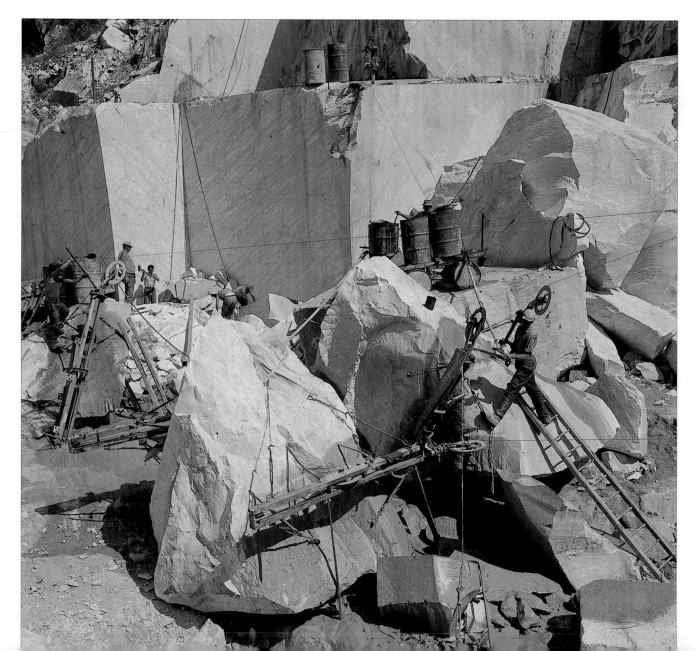

▼ A modern-day marble quarry in Italy. White marble is the most beautiful and expensive building stone. The Romans used it for its decorative qualities, to build the lower seating, and to line the inside walls of the Colosseum.

The Colosseum needed deep foundations to provide a firm base for its high walls. The architects had the clever idea of draining the lake of Nero's Golden House to use as the site of the amphitheater. This was much easier than digging the foundations from scratch. So Nero's lake was emptied and a vast oval ring of concrete was poured in—167 ft. (51 m) wide and 40 ft. (12 m) deep.

While the concrete workers were making the foundations, another workforce was busy 10 mi. (17 km) to the northeast of Rome. They were the stoneworkers, and it was

Concrete

Concrete was invented by the Romans. It was cheap, quick to make, and easy to use. To make concrete, the Romans dropped pieces of rubble into sticky mortar made of lime (a powder of burned chalk or limestone), water, and pozzolana (a volcanic ash). The mortar hardened as it dried, holding the concrete together. Rubble gives concrete its strength. Big lumps of heavy rubble were used in the Colosseum's foundations. Small lumps of light rubble were used in the upper walls.

their job to cut the limestone blocks at the quarries. It was back-breaking work. There were no machines or explosives, and every block had to be cut by hand. The stoneworkers' main tool was a saw with no teeth. Sand was poured beneath the saw's blade, and the stone was slowly ground away.

The stone was taken to Rome on carts pulled by oxen. It has been estimated that 292,000 cartloads of stone were needed for the Colosseum.

▲ A road had to be specially built for transporting stone from the quarries to Rome. This model shows a Roman surveyor using an instrument called a groma to plot a straight road.

1. Scaffolding
2. Seating
3. Arch
4. Corinthian column
5. Walkway
6. Statue
7. Ionic column
8. Doric column
9. Crane with treadwheel
10. Underground passage
11. Cart with stone

◄ It took hundreds of workers eight years to build the Colosseum. This picture shows several different stages of its construction.

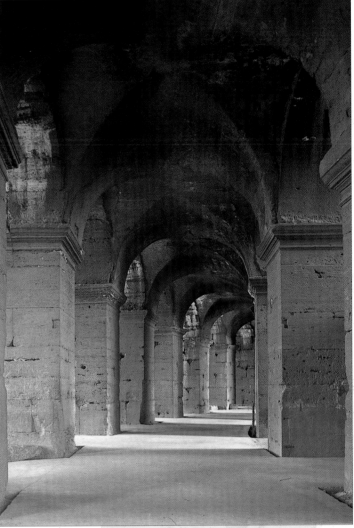

Stone was used on the outside walls and the sections of the building that took the most weight. Huge lifting cranes hoisted stone blocks into the air. They were powered by slaves walking around and around a treadwheel. Inside walls and underground passages were built using heavy concrete and brick. The upper levels were built with less heavy materials, such as wood, bricks, and the lightest concrete.

The outside walls were decorated with Greek columns; a different sort of column was used on each of the three lower levels. Between the columns were statues of gods and heroes, placed beneath the arches around the outside walls. On the topmost level, builders hung large bronze shields, reminding people that this building was a place for combat.

The Colosseum was opened in A.D. 80 by the Emperor Titus, with a hundred days of games. Building work continued on the top levels for a few years. The uppermost tier of columns was added by Titus's brother Domitian two years later, when he had become emperor. The completed building, at 187 ft. (57 m) high, towered over the center of the city.

Arches and vaults
Arches were one of the main features of Roman architecture. They were built over a wooden frame that supported the stones or bricks until they were all in place. A vault is an extended arch built to form a passage or room. This arched walkway goes around the Colosseum on the first floor.

CHAPTER FOUR

THE GREAT SHOW

There was always great excitement before a show in the Colosseum. The events were advertised with colorful signs painted on the walls, which described the attractions and listed the names of the starring gladiators. Heralds walked through the streets shouting announcements.

▼ Early on the morning of a show, crowds of Romans entered the Colosseum. There were 76 entrances and many numbered sections. These made it possible for people to find their way quickly to their seats.

The show often began at dawn with music from an orchestra. The Romans were early risers. From all corners of Rome, 50,000 people made their way to the Colosseum. Entrance to the show was free, like all Roman entertainments, but only those who had been given tickets were allowed in. These ivory tokens, called tesserae, were carved with the numbers of their seats, rows, and sections.

◄ This mosaic from a Roman villa in Germany shows musicians entertaining an audience in an amphitheater.

Seating was arranged according to class. The emperor sat with his family in a marble box in the front row. Also in the front row were the most important people, such as senators and priestesses. Just above were lesser nobles and other wealthy citizens. The ordinary male citizens sat in the second tier. The third tier, hidden from below by a wall, was for women only. All the way at the top there was standing room for noncitizens, slaves, and foreign visitors to the city.

Togas
Romans wore their smartest clothes for a show at the Colosseum. For male citizens this meant putting on a toga, a woolen robe made from an oval piece of cloth about three times as long as the wearer was tall. It was arranged in complicated folds and draped around the body. Senators and important noblemen, such as this consul, wore white togas with a broad purple stripe. Equestrians had a narrow purple stripe on theirs, while ordinary citizens wore plain togas.

Keeping cool
As the sun rose in the sky, the audience was protected by the huge linen velarium, or shade, which hung from poles on the topmost level. It was managed by a team of sailors, chosen for their skill in handling sails and ropes. They shifted it to follow the movement of the sun, so the crowd was always shaded while the arena was brightly lit.

The opening events were lighthearted, designed to warm up the audience. There were fights between old gladiators armed with dummy weapons. Also women, using wooden swords, sometimes fought in the mornings though some Romans found this shocking.

Morning was also the time for tricks by performing animals. Lions caught hares in their mouths and then released the creatures without hurting them. Elephants danced, juggled, wrote letters in the sand with their trunks, and even walked the tightrope. Pliny the Elder, a Roman writer, was amazed at the behavior of one elephant: "It is a known fact that one elephant, somewhat slow in learning its tricks, was often beaten with a lash by its trainer. In the middle of the night, this elephant was found to be practicing its lessons!"

As the different events were taking place, the amphitheater staff was busy shifting scenery and animals.

▶ This stone carving from the British Museum shows two women gladiators fighting in a Roman amphitheater in Greece. Female gladiators were outlawed in A.D. 200 because of public disapproval.

The floor of the arena was made of movable wooden sections over the labyrinth of passages and rooms below. Stage sets and cages containing animals could be hoisted with pulleys directly into the sand-covered arena.

The emperor was part of the entertainment. Every now and then, he would stand up and throw colored balls into the crowd. People who caught these could exchange them for prizes such as baskets of food or gold coins.

"He urged the audience to enjoy themselves, calling them all 'my lords,' and cracking stupid and far-fetched jokes."

The historian Suetonius, describing the Emperor Claudius at a show

▼ The remains of the underground passages and rooms of the Colosseum. This is where animals and prisoners spent their last hours before being brought into the arena.

After watching the tightrope-walking elephants and the fights with dummy weapons, the audience was ready to see some real blood. It was time to bring out the wild beasts from their dark cages beneath the floor of the Colosseum.

The wild beasts took part in different types of entertainment. Fierce animals, such as bulls and rhinos, were made to fight each other. They also fought with the bestiarii, skilled animal fighters armed with spears or bows.

This was also the time for public executions. People found guilty of murder or robbery were tied to stakes mounted in carts and wheeled by attendants toward angry lions and tigers. The attendants carried whips and burning torches, to protect themselves and to drive the animals toward the victims.

The animals themselves were often as terrified as the criminals. They had spent the night in a small, dark cage and now suddenly found themselves in the bright sunlight, surrounded by thousands of shouting people. Some tried to get back into their cages.

This ivory carving and the one opposite show bestiarii, armed only with spears, fighting lions in the arena.

There was an intermission at midday, when many people went out to eat a light lunch. Those who stayed could watch criminals who were forced to kill each other with swords. The writer Seneca described the shouts of the crowd at lunchtime: "'Kill him! Flog him! Burn him! Why does he run at the other man's weapon in such a cowardly way? Why isn't he more keen on dying?' And whenever there's a break they shout, 'Let's have some throats cut in the meantime, so that there's something happening!'"

▲ A beast hunt is staged in the amphitheater to entertain the crowd. The bestiarii attack the leopards with their spears. The central figure is a herald, carrying a tray with moneybags for the victorious huntsmen.

Roman emperors needed vast numbers of animals for their shows. When the Colosseum opened in A.D. 80, 5,000 beasts were killed on a single day. Twenty years later, the Emperor Trajan celebrated a victory by having 11,000 animals killed in the Colosseum.

The Romans hunted animals in every country they had conquered. Wild animals were much more common in Roman times than they are today. Much of Europe was still covered with forests, where wolves and bears lived. In North Africa and the Middle East, you could still find lions and leopards. Elephants were still found in North Africa. These animals, and many others, were brought from the forests to die in amphitheaters all over the empire.

Lands outside the empire also supplied animals. The rulers of India sent tigers and elephants as gifts to the

▶ A farmer carries his harvested produce while a lion lurks nearby. All over the empire, ordinary people were delighted as wild animals were hunted into extinction. Life felt much safer for farmers and shepherds.

Roman emperor. The people of Scotland caught bears
and traded them with the Romans for luxury goods.

In time, the Roman hunts had a terrible effect on these
animals. Elephants began to disappear from North Africa.
Lions were wiped out in Mesopotamia (present-day Iraq).
It became more and more difficult to find wild beasts for
the amphitheaters.

The animals were kept in a zoo by Rome's eastern gate.
On the night before a show, they were driven into crates
and taken by wagons to the Colosseum, where they were
locked in cages below the arena.

▲ The Romans became
expert at hunting,
transporting, and
taking care of
thousands of wild
animals. The beasts
were brought by road
and by sea from all
parts of the empire.
This mosaic shows an
antelope being led up
a gangplank and onto
the ship that will take
the animal to Rome.

CHAPTER FIVE

THE GLADIATORS

In the middle of the afternoon, the part of the show that everyone had been waiting for was announced with a loud trumpet blast. Excitement grew as people realized that the gladiators would soon be fighting. They gambled money, betting on their favorites.

The gladiators walked in a procession into the arena, dressed in brightly colored robes. They marched toward the emperor's box and greeted him, shouting, "Hail Emperor, we who are about to die salute you!" Then the weapons were handed out. The men took off their robes and got ready to fight.

▶ A mosaic showing a victorious gladiator crouching next to his dead opponent. Next to the fighters is an umpire in a white tunic, who is acclaiming the winner.

Helmets and armor

Gladiators were armed in a variety of ways. The Thracian had a short, curved sword and a tiny, round shield. The hoplomachus held a straight sword and crouched behind a long, curved shield. Some wore body armor designed to protect the gladiator from light wounds to his limbs that might keep him from fighting. The chest, where an injury would kill, was usually unprotected. Myrmillo gladiators, who often fought the net-men, had bronze fish mounted on their huge helmets.

Both these helmets were worn by gladiators. Some helmets formed complete masks over the gladiators' faces.

The fight continued until one man was killed or asked for mercy. If his appeal was turned down by the emperor, he was expected to kneel on the ground and allow his throat to be cut without complaining.

Attendants, dressed as underworld gods, approached each fallen gladiator. One carried a red-hot iron to prod him to make sure that he was not pretending to be dead. The other held a huge hammer with which to finish him off. Once they were certain he was dead, they dragged his body out through the Gate of Libitina, goddess of death, to be stripped of his armor. The bloodstained sand was raked over, and the next fight could begin.

There were various ways of ending up as a gladiator. It was a punishment given to criminals and to slaves who had upset their owners. Foreign prisoners, captured in wars, were also sent to fight in the amphitheater.

Sometimes, free men willingly became gladiators. Some were desperate, unable to think of any other way to live. They knew that they would be well fed, and they might only have to fight two or three times a year. Others simply liked fighting. Many gladiators won their freedom only to sign on again when they missed the excitement of the arena and the cheers of the crowds. When a free man became a gladiator, he had to swear a solemn oath that he would allow himself to be "burned by fire, chained, whipped with rods, and killed by the sword." This meant that his trainer could do whatever he liked with him.

▼ This stone carving is part of a triumphal arch celebrating Roman victory over the Gauls. Roman soldiers are holding captured weapons, and their prisoners can be seen below. Some of these foreign captives might have been sent to fight as gladiators.

The gladiators were housed in barracks next to the Colosseum. The barracks had a small arena for training, which was surrounded by rooms for living in. Much of the gladiators' time was spent practicing with wooden weapons. As well as learning to fight, gladiators were trained not to show fear or pain. Nothing was more disgraceful for a gladiator than to cry out if he was wounded.

Successful gladiators could earn a lot of money in prizes. They were treated much like today's celebrities.

▶ A bronze statue of a gladiator, one of the most popular subjects in Roman art. The rewards for a successful gladiator were fame and glory, but gladiators paid a high price in surrendering their freedom and often their lives.

"Celadus, glory of the girls, makes all the girls sigh."

Graffiti about a celebrated retiarius, found at the Roman town of Pompeii

▲ Superstitious gladiators chose certain gods for particular worship. This silver statue shows Fortuna, goddess of good luck, who was their favorite. The gladiators also took stage names that they hoped would bring them luck, such as Victor (Winner) and Celadus (Applause).

33

Roman emperors were always looking for new ways to entertain the public. There was a danger that people would grow bored by seeing the same animals being hunted, the same types of gladiator fighting, and the same type of criminal executions.

One show that was always popular was a mock sea battle. The Emperor Domitian decided to mount a sea battle inside the Colosseum itself. The floor of the arena was waterproofed with canvas. Water was piped in to flood the amphitheater, deeply enough to carry full-size warships. The sight of ships floating inside the building must have been astonishing.

Mock sea battles were rarely put on because they were so expensive. They needed warships manned by thousands of gladiators. The aim was to reenact a famous sea battle from history, such as one fought between the Greeks and the Persians. The gladiators who performed had to dress as Greek and Persian warriors.

◀ A coin showing a Roman galley similar to the ones used in mock sea battles

For the men forced to take part, there was nothing "staged" about a mock sea battle. They fought to the death. The warships, powered by oarsmen, sped across the water, trying to ram and sink each other. Gladiators stood on deck, ready to leap on board a rival ship for hand-to-hand fighting.

In A.D. 52, 19,000 gladiators took part in a sea battle staged by the Emperor Claudius. It was described by the historian Tacitus: "There was energetic rowing, skillful steering, charging, and all the incidents of a sea battle. Though the fighters were criminals, they fought like brave men. After much bloodletting, the survivors were spared."

▲ A 17th-century engraving showing the strange spectacle of an amphitheater flooded for a battle. The arena was not really big enough for the warships to move around or build up speed. Mock sea battles in Rome usually took place on a lake, specially built for the purpose beside the Tiber River. The lake was three times the size of the Colosseum floor and much more effective.

Today people often find it hard to understand why the Romans enjoyed watching people killing each other. In many ways, the Romans were just like us. How could they have enjoyed the shows in the Colosseum?

Every Roman grew up surrounded by images of gladiators. Children played with gladiator dolls. Even babies' bottles had gladiators pictured on them for luck. The idea was that the baby would drink in the fighter's strength with the milk. People decorated their homes with pictures of gladiators fighting and criminals being torn apart by lions.

Most Romans saw nothing cruel or wrong in the games. They believed that it was a good thing to kill criminals and dangerous animals. It was also sensible to do it in public, to show everyone that crimes were punished. People in the audience found this reassuring. They did not question whether it was right, but simply enjoyed the show, swept along by the exciting atmosphere.

◀ Reminders of gladiators were everywhere. Familiar household objects, like this Roman oil lamp, were carved with images of gladiators.

Some Romans were completely obsessed by the games and gladiators. The most famous was Commodus, who was emperor from A.D. 180 to A.D. 192. Although he was ruler of a vast empire, his real interest was in fighting as a gladiator. He appeared in the Colosseum as a wild beast fighter and as a secutor, fighting the net-men. He killed animals for practice in his palace and had his own room in the gladiators' barracks next to the Colosseum.

The huge statue of the sun-god, which stood next to the Colosseum, was converted into a statue of Commodus. Inside the building, Commodus had the arena divided by walls topped with a platform, from which he could fire arrows at the animals from a safe distance. During one show, he killed a hundred bears from his platform. Sometimes he went down into the arena and killed animals, including tigers and elephants.

Roman emperors were not supposed to behave like this. Commodus's closest companions decided to kill him. On New Year's Eve, A.D. 192, the gladiator-emperor was strangled while taking his bath.

▲ Commodus modeled himself on Hercules, the legendary strong man and hunter. This statue shows Commodus in a lion's skin and carrying a club, as Hercules did.

"We senators always had to be there when the emperor (Commodus) was fighting. We would shout whatever we were told, and especially these words continually: 'You are the lord and you are the best! You are the victor and always will be!'"

Dio Cassius, a Roman senator

▼ The Romans worshiped many different gods. When they conquered a country, they welcomed its gods into their own religion. They thought that the more gods you had on your side, the better. This beautiful mosaic shows Romans performing religious rites to the gods of the Nile River in Egypt.

CHAPTER SIX

THE END OF THE GAMES

About the year A.D. 107, a man named Ignatius was on his way from Syria to Rome. He had been arrested for being a Christian, a follower of the new religion that was spreading throughout the Roman Empire at the time. The Christians were the first to speak out against the cruelty and killing of the games. It was against the law to be a Christian, and the punishment was death.

◀ A 19th century engraving showing Ignatius as he was thrown to the lions in the Colosseum

Ignatius was being taken to Rome to be fed to the lions in the Colosseum. Unlike most people in this situation, Ignatius was happy. He wrote: "How I look forward to the lions that have been got ready for me!... I shall encourage them to eat me quickly.... If they refuse, I will force them to do it...splintering of bone and mangling of limb...let every horrid and devilish torture come upon me, if only I may win my way to Jesus Christ!"

The Romans were usually happy to let people follow any religion that they wished to. The problem with the Christians was that they would only worship one god. They believed that all the Roman gods were devils, and they would not pray or make offerings to them. The Romans worried that the Christians' behavior would make the gods angry. The gods would punish everyone for the lack of respect shown by the Christians.

Christians were blamed for every disaster. A Christian writer called Tertullian wrote that if there was a famine or a plague, the cry was always, "the Christians to the lions!" However, the Christians believed that by dying publicly for their beliefs, they would go straight to heaven and encourage others to join them. So they stood in the arena, waving their arms to attract the wild beasts. This behavior and strength of faith baffled the crowd watching the show.

Eusebius, a Christian writer, described the scene in the amphitheater: "Nothing could be more amazing than the fearless courage of these saints... You would see a youngster not yet twenty standing without chains, spreading out his arms in the form of a cross, not budging in the least, though bears and panthers breathing fury and death almost touched his very flesh."

▶ A stone carving of the Roman games showing a man, possibly a Christian, who has been thrown to the lions to be devoured.

Christians were killed for more than 200 years by the Romans, but nothing could stop the spread of their religion. The turning point came in A.D. 312, when Constantine became emperor. He was himself a Christian, and he gave his fellow believers freedom of worship. No more Christians would be thrown to the lions.

This was not enough for the Christians, who wanted all killing in the amphitheaters stopped. In A.D. 404, a monk called Telemachus jumped into the arena to try to stop a gladiatorial fight. A riot started and Telemachus was torn to pieces by the angry crowd. The Emperor Honorius used this as an excuse to ban all fights between gladiators. After 300 years, the killing was over.

▲ A painting of the Emperor Constantine, known as Constantine the Great, with his mother, Saint Helena. According to legend, Saint Helena discovered the cross on which Christ was crucified in the Holy Land, where she was founding churches.

CHAPTER SEVEN

AFTER THE GAMES

▼ In the 1400s the Colosseum became a quarry—a wonderful source of stone and other building materials. Bits of the Colosseum are now spread all over Rome, in palaces, churches, and walls built at the time.

When gladiator fights were banned in A.D. 404, the Roman Empire was already falling apart. Warlike German tribes were pouring over the borders and overpowering Rome's armies. By A.D. 410, Rome itself had been captured.

Despite everything, life in Rome went on, and animal shows were still staged in the Colosseum. With the empire gone, it was much harder to find wild beasts. Instead, farm animals such as bulls and horses were used. The last beast show was held in the year A.D. 523.

Over time, the Colosseum has come to have a different meaning for different groups of people. In 1144 it was turned into a fortress by a Roman family. From the 1200s to the 1400s, the Colosseum was used at various times to stage religious plays. In the 1400s, there were bullfights in the arena. From the 1700s, Catholics came to see the Colosseum as a holy place because of all the Christians who had died there for their faith. A cross was set up in the center of the arena, and Catholics went to pray there.

By the 1800s, the Colosseum had become completely overgrown. The botanist Richard Deakin found 420 different species of plants growing there. In the late 1800s, all the plants were removed by the Italians, who were restoring the ruin. They cleared away the earth and revealed the tunnels beneath the arena. The Colosseum became the tourist sight that we see today.

It is now more than 1,500 years since the last gladiators fought and died inside the walls of the Colosseum. Since then, it has been shaken by seven earthquakes and used as a quarry. Yet the amphitheater still stands, reminding us of the power of the Emperor Vespasian who built it and the thousands of people and animals who died within its walls.

"Never in its bloodiest prime can the sight of the gigantic Colosseum, full and running over with the lustiest life, have moved one heart, as it must move all who look upon it now, a ruin. God be thanked: a ruin!"

The writer Charles Dickens in *Pictures from Italy*, 1844

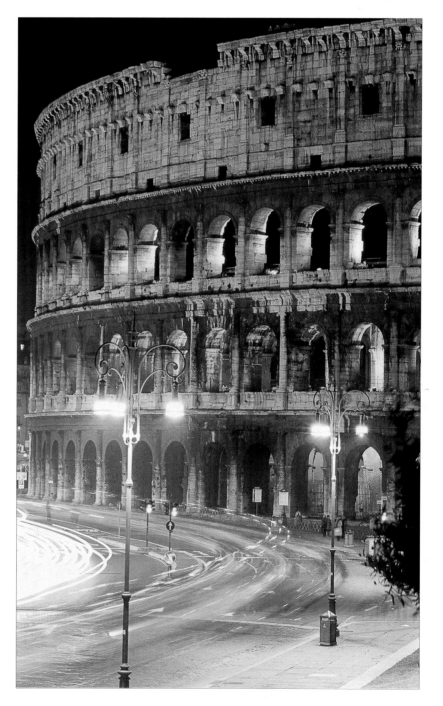

▼ The Colosseum survives today in the center of the busy city of Rome. But the remaining stonework is being damaged by heavy pollution from traffic and industry.

TIME LINE

73–1 B.C.	A.D. 1–199	A.D. 200–399	A.D. 400–599	A.D. 600–799

73–71 Unsuccessful uprising by slaves in southern Italy, led by the gladiator, Spartacus

29 First stone amphitheater built in Rome

54–68 Rule of the Emperor Nero

64 Great fire in Rome

69 After 18 months of civil war, Vespasian becomes emperor

72 Building of the Colosseum begins

80 Opening of the Colosseum

180–192 Rule of Commodus, who fights in the Colosseum as a gladiator

200 Women banned from fighting as gladiators

217 After being struck by lightning, the wooden floor of the amphitheater catches fire

313 Emperor Constantine ends the killing of Christians in the amphitheaters

392 Worship of the old gods banned. Only Christianity is now allowed

404 Emperor Honorius bans gladiatorial games

410 Rome captured and plundered by the Goths, a German people

476 Last western emperor overthrown

523 Last animal games held in the Colosseum

600 Colosseum becomes overgrown

44

A.D. 800–999	A.D. 1000–1199	A.D. 1200–1399	A.D. 1400–1599	A.D. 1600–1900
800 Christians begin pilgrimages to Rome and visit Colosseum	**1144** Colosseum becomes a military stronghold for a powerful Roman family	**1263** Religious plays put on in the Colosseum **1332** Bullfights staged in the Colosseum	**1450s** Colosseum used as a quarry for building materials	**1744** Memorial cross to martyred Christians erected in Colosseum **1871** Italians begin to restore the Colosseum

GLOSSARY

Amphitheater
An oval building for public shows, especially gladiator and wild beast fights. The name means "place for viewing from all sides."

Arena
The fighting area inside an amphitheater. The word itself means "sand."

Bestiarii
Beast fighters: Either skilled gladiators who fought wild animals or criminals condemned to be eaten by them.

Equestrians
Men who belonged to the second most powerful class of Roman nobles.

Games
Free public shows, including chariot races, theatrical performances, and gladiator fights.

Gladiator
Someone who fought in the amphitheater.

Hoplomachus
A gladiator who had a long shield and a straight sword and wore some protective armor.

Secutor
"Pursuer"—a type of gladiator who fought against the net-men.

Thracian
A gladiator who carried a short, curved sword and a small shield.

Retiarius
"Net-man"—a gladiator armed with a net and a trident (three-pronged fishing spear).

Senators
Men who belonged to the richest and most powerful class of Roman nobles. They acted as the emperor's advisers; they commanded armies; and they governed areas of the empire.

Velarium
Linen cloth attached to masts to provide shelter from the sun for the crowd in an amphitheater.

FURTHER INFORMATION

BOOKS

Clare, John D., ed. *Classical Rome*. Living History. Orlando, FL: Harcourt Brace & Co., 1993.

Gardner, Robert. *Architecture*. Yesterday's Science, Today's Technology. New York: 21st Century Books, 1994.

Hicks, Peter. *The Romans*. Look Into the Past. New York: Thomson Learning, 1994.

McKeever, Susan. *Ancient Rome*. DK Pockets. New York: Dorling Kindersley, 1995.

Pratt, Paula B. *Architecture*. World History. San Diego: Lucent Books, 1995.

Singer Donna. *Structures That Changed the Way the World Looked*. Twenty Events. Austin, TX: Raintree Steck-Vaughn, 1994.

Picture acknowledgments

The publishers would like to thank the following for allowing their pictures to be reproduced: Lesley and Roy Adkins: 7 (bottom), 23 (top), 32; Archivi Alinari: 37; Ancient Art & Architecture Collection: pages 7 (top), 11, 13 (bottom), 17 (bottom), 27 (left), 28, 30, 33 (right), 34, 36, 40; Bridgeman Art Library/Prado: page 42; British Museum: pages 24, 33 (left); Colchester Museums: page 4; C M Dixon Photo Resources: pages 19, 26, 27 (right); ET Archive: pages 12, 14, 38, 41; Mary Evans Picture Library: pages 8 (bottom), 39; Werner Forman Archive: pages 13 (top), 15; Sonia Halliday Photographs: pages 18, 29; Robert Harding Picture Library: page 11 (top); Michael Holford Photographs: pages 10, 23 (bottom); Angelo Hornak Photograph Library: page 8 (top), 21; Image Bank: front cover (Alan Becker); pages 17 (top), 22; Impact Photos: page 25; Mansell Collection: page 35; Tony Stone Images: pages 9, 43; Wayland Picture Library: pages 3, 31, 44-45.

INDEX

Numbers in **bold** refer to illustrations.

amphitheaters 4, 9, 11, **11**, 14, 15, 34, 35, 43
animals 10, **11**, 19
  hunting 28–29
  performing 24–25, 26
  sacrificial 10
  transport **29**
  wild 26, **26**, **27**, 28–29, **28**, **29**, 36, 39, **39**, 40, **40**, 42
arches, 20, 21, **21**
architect 16–17
arena 4–5, **4–5**, 24, 29, 30
audience 4, **4**, 16, 23, 24, 25, 26

barracks 33
bestiarii 26, **26**, **27**
botany 43
builders 6, 8, 17
building materials 17
  brick 21
  concrete 18, 19, 21
  limestone 19, 21
  marble **18**
  wood 21

chariot racing 8, 10, **10**
Christianity 38–41
  attitudes to 39–41
Christians 38–41
  killing of **39**, **40**, 42
citizens 7, **7**, 23
Claudius *see* emperors
coins **13**
Commodus *see* emperors
Constantine *see* emperors
construction 16, 17, 18–19, 20–21, **20**
craftspeople 6, 17, **17**, 18, 19
criminals 26, 27, 36

Domitian *see* emperors

earthquakes 43
emperors
  at the games 5, **5**, 23, 25, 30
  Claudius 25, 35
  Commodus 37, **37**
  Constantine 41, **41**
  Domitian 14, 21, 34
  funding shows 10, 11
  Galba **13**
  gifts to 29
  Honorius 41
  Nero 12–13, **12**, 13, 14, 15
  Otho **13**
  Titus 14, 15, **15**, 21
  Trajan 28
  Vespasian 14, **14**, 15, 16, 43
  Vitellius **13**
entertainment 10–11, 25, 34

farmer **28**
Fortuna **33**
Forum **8**, **9**
foundations 18

games 21, 36, 38
  attitudes to 36, 37
gladiators 4–5, **4–5**, 11, 16, 32–33, **33**, 34, 35, 41
  armor 4, 31, **31**
  death of **30**, 31
  fame of 33, 36
  women 24, **24**
gods 7, 8, 10, 21, 31, **33**, 38, 39
Golden House 12–13, **13**, 14
guilds 17

Honorius *see* emperors

Ignatius 38, 39, **39**

mock sea battles 34, 35, **35**
musicians 10, 23, **23**

Nero *see* emperors

plan 14, **14**
pollution 43
prisoners 25, 32

quarries **18**, 19, **42**, 43

roads 8, 19
Roman empire 6–7, 28
  map **6**
Rome 6, 14, 15
  buildings 8–9, **8**
  capture of 42
  entertainments in 10, 11
  fire and rebuilding 12, 13

sacrifice 7, 10, 11
Saint Helena **41**
seating 16, 18, 23
show 22, 24–27, 30
slaves 7, **7**, 10, 11, 17, 21
soldiers 6, 10, 13, 32
Stadium of Domitian **8**

Telemachus 41
temples 8
tickets 23
Titus *see emperors*
togas 23, **23**
traffic 43, **43**

velarium 24
Vespasian *see* emperors

war 6, 10, 13
warships 34, 35
worship 38, **38**, 39